MAR 0 8 2010

P9-DGE-970

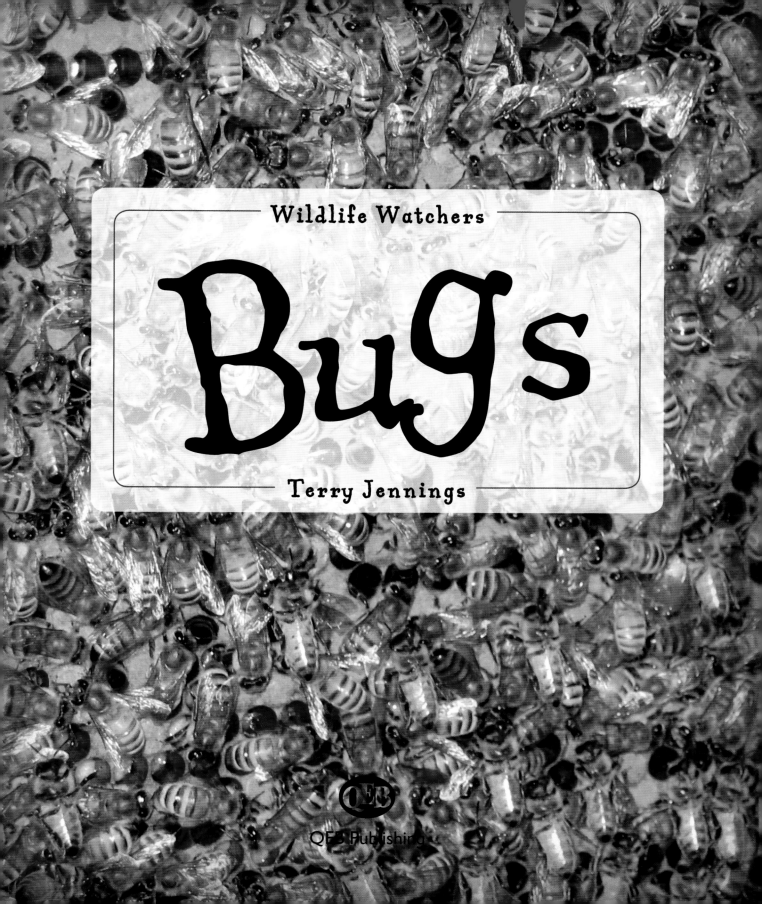

# Wildlife Watchers

# Bugs

Terry Jennings

QEB Publishing

Published in the United States by
QEB Publishing, Inc.
3 Wrigley, Suite A
Irvine, CA 92618

www.qeb-publishing.com

Library of Congress Cataloging-in-Publication Data

Jennings, Terry J.
  Bugs / Terry Jennings.
    p. cm. -- (QEB wildlife watchers)
  Includes index.
  ISBN 978-1-59566-757-1 (hardcover)
  1. Invertebrates--Juvenile literature. 2. Insects--
Juvenile literature. I. Title. II. Series: QEB wildlife
watchers.
  QL362.4.J46 2010
  595.7--dc22

                              2009005882

Printed and bound in China

**Author** Terry Jennings
**Consultant** Steve Parker
**Project Editor** Eve Marleau
**Designer and Picture Researcher**
    Liz Wiffen

**Publisher** Steve Evans
**Creative Director** Zeta Davies
**Managing Editor** Amanda Askew

**Picture credits**
Key: t=top, b=bottom, r=right, l=left, c=center

**Alamy** 5tr Harry Taylor, 19l blickwinkel/
MeulvanCauteren

**DK Images** 27l Dave King

**NHPA** 11l N A Callow, 13t Laurie Campbell, 13c
Joe Blossom, 21t Stephen Dalton, 27t Eric Soder,
27b Image Quest 3-D

**Photolibrary** 13b, 28b Andoni Canela

**Shutterstock** 2–3 PhotoLiz, 3r Cre8tive Images, 4t
Robert Taylor, 4b Alex Kuzovlev, 4–5c Dusty Cline,
5tc Yaroslav, 5b Steve McWilliam, 6–7t Johanna
Goodyear, 6–7c Morgan Lane Photography, 9t
Steve McWilliam, 9c Lepas, 10c Cre8tive Images,
11c Robert Taylor, 11r Yaroslav, 12b Christian
Musat, 14l Joseph Calev, 14r Yellowj, 15c Palto, 15r
Dole, 16t Florin Tirlea, 16c Studiotouch, 17b Dave
Massey, 18c Kurt G, 19b Andrey Pavlov, 19r Andrey
Armyagov, 20–21 vnlit, 21r Kurt G, 22–23t Joseph
Calev, 23rt Joseph Calev, 23rb Joseph Calev,
23bl Steve McWilliam, 24c Alex Kuzovlev, 25c
Christopher Tan Teck Hean, 25b Scott Rothstein,
27b Dusty Cline, 26–27b Christoph Weihs, 26b
design56, 28t Lucio Tamino Hollander Correia, 29t
vera bogaerts, 29c Dave Massey, 29r Tiplyashin
Anatoly, 32 PhotoLiz.

**StockXchange** 8–9 Peranandham Ramaraj,
10–11 Dawn Allynn, 22–23 Stephen Eastop

The words in **bold** are explained
in the glossary on page 30.

# Contents

# What is a bug?

Bugs are some of the smallest animals in the world. Whether you live in the countryside or in a city, there are always bugs somewhere nearby. They live on land, in water, and soil, and even in our homes.

Cranefly

Beetle

Butterfly

Slug

## No backbone

Scientists call bugs by their proper name, which is **invertebrate** animals. They are small animals that do not have a backbone inside their body. Some bugs, such as snails and beetles, have a shell or hard wings to protect them. Others, such as earthworms, have no protection at all.

Earthworm

Snail

# Insects

Most of the animals we call bugs are insects. They have six legs and a body divided into three parts. For example, a wasp is an insect. Spiders, centipedes, millipedes, woodlice, slugs, snails, and earthworms are not insects because they do not have a body like this.

## Did you know?

There are more than one million different **species**, or kinds, of insect. The heaviest insect is the African Goliath beetle, which can weigh up to 3.5 ounces (100 grams).

Antenna    Head    Thorax

Wing

Eye

Mouthparts

# Body parts

Insects have three main parts to their body—the head, thorax, and abdomen. The brain, eyes, and mouthparts are all in the head. The wings and legs are attached to the insect's thorax. The abdomen is where the digestive system and heart are placed. Some insects, such as female bees and wasps, also have a sting at the end of their abdomen.

Leg

Abdomen

Sting

⬆ Like all insects, this wasp has six legs. It also has two pairs of wings.

Woodlouse

5

# Be a bug hunter

Bugs are rather small, so you need to get close to them to see all their details. This should be avoided with bugs that sting, such as bees and wasps. One way to get a good look at bugs is to use a magnifying glass or hand lens.

⬇ A magnifying glass lets you see small things much more clearly.

## The bug-hunter's collecting kit

These are the main tools you will need for bug hunting:

- Magnifying glass
- Plastic jars and margarine or ice-cream tubs, with air-holes in the lids
- Small paintbrushes and plastic spoons for picking up bugs without hurting them
- Notebook
- Pen or pencil
- Crayons

⬆ Plastic jars are good if you can make little air-holes in the lid.

➡ If you see a bug you do not recognize, draw a sketch.

## Keeping records

Every bug hunter needs a notebook, some pencils, and crayons. Once you have found a bug you can put its details in a table.

| Date | Type of bug | Time of day | Place | Kind of weather | Where was the bug? | What was the bug doing? |
|------|-------------|-------------|-------|-----------------|--------------------|--------------------------|
| April 28 | Honeybee | 11 a.m. | In the park | Sunny | On snapdragon flower | Collecting pollen |
| May 2 | Ant | 3:20 p.m. | Sidewalk | Sunny | In cracks in sidewalk | Carrying sand |
| July 18 | Snail | 6 p.m. | Yard | Raining | On cabbage plant | Feeding on leaf |
|  |  |  |  |  |  |  |
|  |  |  |  |  |  |  |
|  |  |  |  |  |  |  |
|  |  |  |  |  |  |  |

**WARNING!**

Do not touch any bug with your bare hands. Release a bug when you have studied it. Always make sure an adult knows where you are.

# Butterflies and moths

## Watch it!

Record which colors and kinds of flower you see butterflies and moths feeding from. Do they have a favorite kind of flower?

Both butterflies and moths have four wings. The front pair are called the **forewings**. The wingspan is the distance between the wing tips.

Am I mostly black with orange or red bands on my wings? Do I have white marks on my forewings?

Orange or red band

White marks

## Spotting butterflies and moths

- There are about 20,000 different kinds of butterfly and 100,000 species of moth.

- Butterfly and moth eggs hatch into caterpillars before they turn into adults. Caterpillars look like worms and have many legs. They can be many different colors, and even have spikes to stop birds from eating them.

- You can tell a butterfly from a moth by looking at its wings when it lands. Most moths land with their wings flat. Butterflies usually hold their wings together, above their body.

## Red admiral butterfly

Wingspan: 2.5 in (64 mm)
Food: Nectar from flowers and juices from fruits
Habitat: Almost anywhere with flowers or stinging nettles
Eggs: Laid on leaves such as nettles

**Am I active in the daytime? Am I mainly black with red markings?**

Red markings

# Cinnabar moth

**Wingspan:** 1.8 in (45 mm)
**Food:** Nectar from flowers
**Habitat:** Yards, parks, waste ground, and farmland
**Eggs:** Laid on the underside of leaves such as ragwort and groundsel

Black tip

**Am I mainly white? Do my forewings have black spots and black tips?**

Black spot

**Am I active at night? Do I have tigerlike white stripes on my forewings?**

White stripes

# Cabbage white butterfly

**Wingspan:** 2.5 in (64 mm)
**Food:** Nectar from flowers
**Habitat:** Near plants
**Eggs:** Laid on the underside of leaves such as cabbages and cauliflowers

# Tiger moth

**Wingspan:** 3 in (76 mm)
**Food:** Nectar from flowers
**Habitat:** Yards, parks, and waste ground
**Eggs:** Laid on the underside of leaves such as nettles and weeds

# Flies

Flies are insects. There are more than 120,000 different kinds of flies in the world. People think that flies are a pest because they buzz around food, and a few can bite. Most flies are actually useful and harmless.

Large eye

## Did you know?

The wings of flies beat very fast. Those of a housefly beat about 200 times a second, a mosquito about 600 times a second, and a midge about 1000 times a second.

Am I medium sized and mainly dark blue or black with large eyes?

## Spotting flies

🪰 Flies have only two proper wings. Their back wings, which are very small, are used for balance as they fly.

🪰 All flies lay eggs, which hatch into grubs or maggots. After spending some time feeding, the grubs turn into **pupae**, and then into adults

## Housefly

**Length:** 0.3 in (8 mm)
**Food:** Almost any kind of food, including human food, rotten fruit, and the contents of garbage bins, animal droppings
**Habitat:** Everywhere
**Eggs:** Laid in manure or waste food or in soil

Am I grey-brown with a long, thin body and narrow wings? Are my legs very long and fragile?

Am I very tiny with large eyes? Am I flying around rotting fruits such as apples and pears?

Is my body covered in yellow-and-black stripes? When I fly, do I hover in one place?

## Cranefly or daddy-long-legs
Length: 0.8 in (20 mm)
Food: Adults rarely feed
Habitat: Fields, parks, and yards. They often come into houses in fall
Eggs: Laid in soil

Narrow wing

Thin body

Large eye

Yellow-and-black stripes

## Fruit fly
Length: 0.2 in (6 mm)
Food: Sugary juices from rotting fruit
Habitat: Yards and orchards
Eggs: Laid in rotting fruit

## Hoverfly
Length: 0.5 in (14 mm)
Food: Nectar from flowers
Habitat: Parks, yards, and farmland
Eggs: Laid on plant leaves

# Beetles

There are more than 370,000 different kinds of beetle in the world. They are found almost everywhere. It is easy to recognize beetles because, unlike other insects, they are covered with tough **wing cases** that look like armor. These cases are the beetle's forewings.

## Spotting beetles

- The back wings of beetles are large and papery. When beetles fly, the forewings are held upward and only the back wings flap.
- Some beetles eat flesh, such as that of other insects. Many more beetles feed on plants and animal dung.

Am I quite small with a narrow body and long antennae? Is my thorax red or black?

Narrow body

Red thorax

## Soldier beetle

**Length:** 0.4 in (10 mm)
**Food:** Small insects
**Habitat:** In large flowers and on the surface of soil
**Eggs:** Laid in groups in soil

Long antenna

Am I long and black or dark blue? Do I have long antennae?

**?**

## Ground beetle
**Length:** 0.6 in (16 mm)
**Food:** Other insects
**Habitat:** On the ground among dead leaves and under logs and stones
**Eggs:** Laid on the ground or just below the surface of soil

**?**

Am I black with orange or yellow stripes running across my body? Am I near the dead body of a small animal?

## Sexton beetle
**Length:** 0.6 in (16 mm)
**Food:** The flesh of dead animals
**Habitat:** Near dead animals
**Eggs:** Laid in the bodies of dead animals

Orange stripe

Am I black with short antennae? Do I have ridges running along my body?

**?**

## Dung beetle
**Length:** 1 in (25 mm)
**Food:** The dung or droppings of animals
**Habitat:** In grassland and where animals such as cows, horses, and rabbits leave their droppings
**Eggs:** Laid in animal droppings

Ridges

# Ladybugs

Ladybugs are probably the best known beetles. Gardeners and farmers like them because they eat pests, such as greenfly and blackfly, that damage the plants in gardens and on farms.

Am I small with short legs? Are my wing cases yellow or orange with black spots, one on each wing case?

← A ladybug will eat large numbers of harmful greenfly and blackfly every day.

Short leg

Large, black spot

## Spotting ladybugs

🐞 Ladybugs are usually brightly colored with dark spots. There are about 5,000 different kinds of ladybugs in the world. Each kind has a different pattern and number of spots.

🐞 If a ladybug is attacked, it will squirt out nasty-smelling blood to protect itself.

🐞 In winter, ladybugs hide away and **hibernate**, or sleep, until the warmer weather returns.

## Two-spot ladybug

**Length:** 0.2 in (6 mm)
**Food:** Tiny insects such as greenfly and blackfly
**Habitat:** Parks, yards, farmland, woodland, waste ground
**Eggs:** About 20 eggs laid on the underside of leaves of plants that are full of greenfly and blackfly

14-spot ladybug

**Length:** 0.2 in (5 mm)
**Food:** Mainly greenfly and blackfly
**Habitat:** Yards, farmland, woodland, waste ground
**Eggs:** 20-50 eggs laid on the underside of leaves of plants that are full of greenfly and blackfly

Am I red or yellow with about 14 black spots, or black with about 14 yellow or red spots?

Do I have short legs? Are my wing cases yellow or orange with black spots? Are the spots almost square?

Red wing case

Seven-spot ladybug

**Length:** 0.3 in (8 mm)
**Food:** Mainly greenfly and blackfly
**Habitat:** Yards, farmland, woodland, waste ground
**Eggs:** Up to 200 eggs on the underside of leaves of plants that are full of greenfly and blackfly

Square spot

**Did you know?**

A seven-spot ladybug can eat up to 30 greenfly or blackfly in 60 minutes. That's one fly every two minutes!

15

# Bees and wasps

Bees and wasps are insects. They feed on sweet nectar from flowers. Wasps can be troublesome in summer when they buzz around sugary foods.

← A beehive has six-sided cells where the eggs and grubs live, and where bees store honey.

← Wasps feed their grubs inside the small cells where they hatch from eggs.

## Spotting bees and wasps

🐝 Each hive, or nest, is home to a large number of bees or wasps and their mother— the **queen**.

🐝 **Pollen** from flowers gets stuck on the bees' hairy coat. The pollen is passed by accident from one flower to another by bees. This **pollinates** the flowers.

🐝 For most of summer, wasps catch and kill insects, which they feed to their grubs.

### Did you know?

Honeybees are good at finding flowers and remembering where they are. When they get back to the hive they do a special dance, which may help to tell the other **worker** bees where to go.

Do I have a fat, hairy body? Am I mainly black with gold, red, or white markings?

Do I have a black body with yellow stripes and black spots?

Black spot

## Common wasp
**Length:** 0.9 in (22 mm)
**Food:** Mostly insects. Ripe fruit and sweet foods in late summer
**Habitat:** Almost everywhere in the town and countryside
**Eggs:** Laid by the queen wasp inside the nest

Fat, hairy body

## Bumble bee
**Length:** 0.7 in (18 mm)
**Food:** Pollen and nectar from flowers
**Habitat:** Yards, parks, farmland, woodland
**Eggs:** Laid by queen bumble bee inside the nest

Yellow stripe

## Honeybee
**Length:** 0.6 in (16 mm)
**Food:** Pollen and nectar from flowers
**Habitat:** Almost anywhere where there are flowers
**Eggs:** Laid by the queen bee inside the hive

## WARNING!
Don't get too close to bees or wasps. They can sting if they feel threatened or see sudden movement.

Am I rather small and mainly black or brown? Do I have an orange band on my abdomen?

Orange band

Pollen

17

# Ants

Ants live in large **colonies**, or groups. There may be 100,000 ants in a colony, but they all have the same mother—the queen ant. The ants that you see most often are the worker ants. These are female ants that are unable to lay eggs.

## Watch it!

Look out for flying ants swarming in the air. These are the males and egg-laying females leaving the nest for their mating flight. After they have mated, the males die, but the females begin to make new nests to lay eggs in.

Am I small and dark brown or black all over?

Dark-brown body

## Spotting ants

- There are about 14,000 different kinds of ants in the world. Ants are insects. Most have a fat abdomen, long legs, and strong jaws.

- The worker ants do not have wings because they live in sheltered nests where wings would get in the way.

- Ants feed on many kinds of food, but most like sweet things. Some ants milk greenfly and blackfly for a sweet liquid, called **honeydew**, that they produce.

## Black garden ant

Length: 0.2 in (5 mm) worker ant
Food: Plants, seeds, small animals, and honeydew
Habitat: Everywhere in the town and countryside
Eggs: Laid in an underground nest by the queen ant

Am I small and yellow-brown in color? Do I live in grassy areas?

## Yellow meadow ant

**Length:** 0.1 in (3 mm) worker ant
**Food:** Plants, seeds, and other small animals
**Habitat:** Grassland. Its nests look like mounds of sand or soil
**Eggs:** Laid underground by the queen ant

Yellow-brown abdomen

Am I small and yellow? Am I inside a house or warm building?

Yellow body

## Wood ant

**Length:** 1.4 in (6 mm) worker ant
**Food:** Plants, seeds, and small animals
**Habitat:** Woodland that has trees with needle-shaped leaves
**Eggs:** Laid by the queen ant in a huge nest made of tree leaves

Am I large with a red thorax and a dark-colored abdomen? Do I live in woodland?

Red thorax

## Pharaoh's ant

**Length:** 0.1 in (2 mm) worker ant
**Food:** Scraps of human food
**Habitat:** In cracks inside warm buildings
**Eggs:** Laid by the queen in nests inside crevices, or cracks, in warm buildings

# Spiders

Spiders feed mainly on insects, many of which are flies. Larger spiders that live in the tropics can catch and eat small birds and mice.

> Am I brown in color with a white cross on my back?

White cross

## Spotting spiders

🪰 All spiders have eight legs and most have eight eyes. Their body has two parts to it—the cephalothorax, a combination of the head and thorax joined together, and the abdomen.

🪰 All spiders can make silk. The silk leaves the spider's body as a liquid, but it hardens as soon as it touches the air. Some spiders use silk to make traps, called webs, to catch their **prey**.

🪰 There are more than 40,000 different kinds of spider.

## Garden spider

**Length:** 0.5 in (13 mm)
**Food:** Small flying insects, which it traps in its web
**Habitat:** Yards, parks, woodland, waste ground, and hedgerows
**Eggs:** Up to 800 eggs are laid on fence posts and in cracks in trees

## Watch it!

Find a spider's web and gently break part of the web with the tip of a blade of grass. Look again the next morning. Has the spider mended its web?

Long leg

**Do I have very long legs? Is my body yellow or red-brown in color with patches on it?**

## House spider

**Length:** 0.4 in (10 mm)
**Food:** Small insects, which it traps in its web
**Habitat:** In buildings
**Eggs:** Laid inside a wrapping of silk inside a building

**Do I have long legs? Do I have a pale stripe down the middle of my cephalothorax?**

Female with an egg sac

Pale stripe

**Am I small, and yellow or white in color? Do I have a fat body and legs that look like a crab's?**

Legs like a crab

Long leg

## Wolf spider

**Length:** 0.3 in (8 mm)
**Food:** Small insects, which it chases
**Habitat:** Bare ground in yards, parks, farmland, and woodland
**Eggs:** Females lay their eggs in a silk ball

## Crab spider

**Length:** 0.4 in (10 mm)
**Food:** Small insects, which it catches by surprise
**Habitat:** Among tall grasses and on flowers
**Eggs:** Females lay eggs in a bag of silk

# Many legs

All insects have six legs, while spiders have eight legs. Some small animals have many more legs than this. They include woodlice, centipedes, and millipedes. These animals can be found hiding in rotting wood, under stones, logs, or heaps of dead tree leaves.

Two legs on each segment

Am I long? Do I have one pair of antennae? Am I made up of segments with two pairs of legs on each?

## Spotting bugs with many legs

- 🪰 A woodlouse has 14 legs and its body is covered with hard plates that overlap like the tiles of a roof.

- 🪰 Centipedes and millipedes are usually much longer than woodlice. Their bodies are made up of segments. Some can have several hundred legs.

- 🪰 Woodlice and millipedes mainly eat dead plants.

- 🪰 Centipedes feed on tiny animals such as insects and their grubs.

## Millipede

Length: 0.8–2 in (20–50 mm)
Food: Dead plants and rotting wood
Habitat: Under logs, stones, bark, and dead leaves
Eggs: Some millipedes lay their eggs in tiny nests

Am I long?
Do I have one
pair of antennae?
Am I made up of
segments with
only one pair
of legs on
each segment?

# Centipede

**Length:** 1–3 in (25–80 mm)
**Food:** Small animals such as insects and their grubs
**Habitat:** Under logs, stones, bark, and heaps of dead leaves
**Eggs:** The female rolls her eggs along the ground so that they look like lumps of soil

Long antenna

Am I mainly gray or
dark brown in color?
Do I sometimes roll up
into a tight ball?

# Pill woodlouse

**Length:** 0.7 in (18 mm)
**Food:** Dead plants, rotting wood
**Habitat:** In damp places, such as under tree bark, logs and stones, and under heaps of rotting leaves
**Eggs:** Laid in the mother's pouch

Gray body

Rolled up

Am I mainly
gray or dark
brown in color?
Do I have 14 legs
and a pair of
long antennae?

Antenna

# Woodlouse

**Length:** 0.7 in (18 mm)
**Food:** Dead plants, rotting wood
**Habitat:** In damp places, such as under tree bark, logs and stones, and under heaps of rotting leaves
**Eggs:** Laid in the mother's pouch

## Did you know?

In Central and South America, centipedes can grow up to 12 inches (30 cm) long. They can give people painful bites.

23

# Look, no legs!

Some animals, such as slugs and snails, have a "foot." The foot is the underside of their body. It is made of tiny muscles that help them to move. Snails are better protected than slugs because they have a shell to help them hide from their enemies or bad weather.

*Is my shell large and rounded? Is it mainly light brown in color and patterned with darker bands?*

## Spotting slugs and snails

- The shell of a snail is made of a chalky material produced by the snail's body. A snail can pull its whole body into the shell, but it can never leave the shell altogether.

- Slugs look like snails without shells, although some slugs have a small shell that is hidden under the skin.

- Both slugs and snails have two pairs of tentacles on their heads. The larger pair has eyes on their tips. The smaller pair of tentacles is used for smelling.

Large shell

### Garden snail
**Shell size:** Up to 1.5 in (38 mm) high and 1.4 in (35 mm) wide
**Food:** Living and dead plants, such as cabbages and lettuces
**Habitat:** Almost anywhere there are plants growing, especially in yards and parks
**Eggs:** Laid in groups in damp soil

Am I large and completely black? Do I sometimes curl up?

Black body

# Great black slug

**Length:** Up to 6 in (15 cm)
**Food:** Plants, droppings
**Habitat:** Parks, woodland, yards, and waste ground
**Eggs:** Laid in clusters in damp soil or compost heaps

Is my shell tiny and almost see-through? Is it cone shaped with a blunt tip?

Cone-shaped shell

# Moss snail

**Shell size:** Up to 0.2 in (6 mm) long and 1 in (3 mm) wide
**Food:** Small plants
**Habitat:** Almost everywhere that is damp, including under dead leaves, logs, and in long grass
**Eggs:** Laid in clusters in damp soil or mossy plants

Am I small and very slimy? Am I gray, light brown, or pale yellow in color?

Slimy body

# Netted slug or field slug

**Length:** Up to 1 in (2.5 cm)
**Food:** Mainly green plants
**Habitat:** Yards, parks, and farmland
**Eggs:** Laid in clusters in damp soil or under stones

## Watch it!

Line an old margarine container with damp paper towels and make air-holes in the lid. Put a snail in it and surround it with different kinds of food such as a piece of apple and potato. Which foods does the snail like best?

# The earthworm

Although they are usually small, earthworms are some of the most important animals in the world. Luckily, there are millions of them. An area the size of a soccer field could be home to five million worms.

**Am I long and thin, with no legs, eyes, or ears? Am I made up of segments with a fatter area, called the saddle, toward the front end?**

Segment

Saddle

Mouth

## Spotting the earthworm

🪰 An earthworm has a head and a tail, but most of its body is made up of segments that are very similar to each other. Each of these segments has a number of small, stiff hairs on it. These help the worm to grip the sides of the burrow that it lives in.

🪰 Worms have no ears, eyes, or nose. Their skin is sensitive to light.

🪰 Worms are very good for soil because their burrows allow air and water to reach plant roots. Their wormcasts, or droppings, help to make the soil more **fertile**.

### Earthworm
**Length:** 1–7 in (3–18 cm)
**Food:** Dead leaves, decaying plants, and animal material
**Habitat:** In soil
**Eggs:** Laid in a little brown bag, or cocoon, about 0.2 in (6 mm) long

Dead tree leaves

← Wormcasts show where earthworms have been feeding during the night.

Colored soil

Earthworm

# Make a wormery

You will need:
- Large, see-through jar
- Small amounts of three different-colored soils
- Piece of cling wrap
- Small amount of sand or chalk
- Sheet of black paper
- Sticky tape
- Dead tree leaves
- Three earthworms

1. Remove any stones or lumps from the soils and put layers of each colored soil in the jar.
2. Next, put a thin layer of sand or chalk on the soils. Add some water to keep the soils moist.
3. Put in the earthworms and lay the dead leaves on the surface.
4. Cover the outside of the jar with black paper. Keep the wormery in a cool, dark place.
5. After a few days, remove the black cover to see what has happened. Record the results.
6. Return the worms to where you found them.

# Bugs in danger

Although bugs seem to be everywhere, many kinds are in danger of dying out altogether. This is called **extinction**. Most are facing extinction because of things that humans do.

## Habitat loss

Every kind of bug lives in particular surroundings. This is its habitat, or home. All over the world, humans are destroying habitats. Marshes and wetlands are being drained, and woods and forests are being cleared to provide land for roads and factories. In many other places, soil that bugs live in is being covered over with concrete and buildings.

⬆ This land is being cleared to make way for a new road. The bugs that live and lay eggs here will have to find somewhere else to go.

⬇ Collections of rare butterflies and moths were once sold for a lot of money.

## Collecting

In some parts of the world, many large butterflies and moths are collected and killed. They are then used to make pictures, or other ornaments, for vacationers to buy as souvenirs.

← The chemical being sprayed on this field may kill the useful bugs as well as the harmful ones.

## Did you know?

More than 1000 different kinds of butterfly are in danger of becoming extinct. In many parts of the world, colonies of honeybees are dying out.

## Pollution

Many bugs have been killed by **pollution**, such as chemicals used on farms to kill pests or to make crops grow better. Often, these chemicals kill useful animals, such as ladybugs and bees, as well as the pests. If the chemicals do not kill the bugs, they may kill the plants that the bugs need for food or to lay their eggs on.

## Watch it!

Everyone can help bugs by making the areas around homes and schools safe for them to lay eggs and feed. Even if you don't have a yard, you can plant pots, tubs or window boxes with the flowers that bees, butterflies, and other insects like to visit.

↑ If you find a bug somewhere where it might get hurt, move it carefully to a safe place.

# Glossary

**Antenna** Feeler on an insect's head used for touching and smelling.

**Colony** A group of animals of a species nesting together.

**Extinction** When something no longer exists. A species is extinct when every member of it has died out.

**Fertile** In a good condition, or full of nutrients, for plants or animals to grow.

**Forewing** The front wing in a pair, or set, of wings.

**Hibernate** To spend winter in a sleepy state.

**Honeydew** A sweet liquid produced by some insects.

**Invertebrate** An animal without a backbone.

**Nectar** Sweet-tasting liquid produced by flowers.

**Pollen** A yellow dust produced by flowers.

**Pollinate** To carry pollen from one flower to another.

**Pollution** Chemicals that make the air, water, soil, or other parts of the environment dirty.

**Prey** An animal hunted and eaten by another animal.

**Pupa** The stage after the grub stage, during which an adult insect develops.

**Queen** A female ant, bee, or wasp that lays eggs.

**Species** Any one kind of animal or plant.

**Wing cases** The hard front wings of beetles.

**Worker** One of the female ants, bees, wasps, or termites that do the work of the colony.

# Index

# Notes for parents and teachers

🐛 The children should be encouraged to treat bugs with care and respect. Any animals caught for study should be set free in the area they were collected when a project is finished.

🐛 A visit to a zoo, wildlife park, natural history museum, or butterfly farm will help to show children the great diversity of wildlife in the world today.

🐛 Before you start, check that the children aren't allergic to any plants or animals.

🐛 A number of safety precautions are necessary when children study invertebrate animals. They should always wash their hands thoroughly after handling small animals, plants, and soil, and particularly before touching food. Similar attention to hygiene is also necessary when cleaning out the boxes in which bugs have been kept.

🐛 Bees, wasps, and ants can give painful stings or bites, so do not go near their nests or hives.

🐛 Buy a bug box and put it in your yard or playground. It will give shelter to insects, such as ladybugs, in winter.

*\* Website information is correct at time of going to press. However, the publishers cannot accept liability for any information or links found on third-party websites.*

🐛 Look for tracks and traces of bugs around your area, such as leaves that have been chewed by butterfly larvae (caterpillars). In damp weather, children might be able to see slug trails on footpaths.

🐛 Visit a wooded area during late summer or early fall. Bugs are most active at this time of the year.

🐛 Some useful websites for more information:
www.kidsplanet.org
www.sciencespot.net
www.butterflywebsite.com
www.kidzone.ws/animals
www.buglife.org.uk/discoverbugs
www.butterflyconservation.org/text/8/learn.html